FOXGLO

ANGE MLINKO

Foxglovewise

faber

First published in the UK in 2025
by Faber & Faber Ltd
The Bindery, 51 Hatton Garden
London EC1N 8HN

First published in the USA in 2025
by Farrar, Straus and Giroux
120 Broadway, New York 10271

Typeset by Hamish Ironside
Printed in the UK by Martins the Printers

The right of Ange Mlinko to be identified as author of this work
has been asserted in accordance with Section 77 of the Copyright,
Designs and Patents Act 1988

Grateful acknowledgment is made for permission to reprint lines
from 'Matins' from *The Wild Iris* by Louise Glück. Copyright © 1992
by Louise Glück. Used by permission of Carcanet Press Limited.

A CIP record for this book is available from the British Library

ISBN 978–0–571–39386–2

2 4 6 8 10 9 7 5 3 1

In memory of my mother and father

. . . are you like the hawthorn tree,
always the same thing in the same place,
or are you more the foxglove, inconsistent, first springing up
a pink spike on the slope behind the daisies,
and the next year, purple in the rose garden?

– LOUISE GLÜCK, 'Matins'

Contents

FOXGLOVEWISE

Tarpon Springs, Epiphany

Every high C accurately struck demolishes the theory
that we are the irresponsible puppets of fate or chance.
— W. H. AUDEN

Maria Callas came to our banal climate, age five,
wearing her first pair of glasses, so that perhaps
the fizz of palms was the first thing to come into focus.

In time she might have seen the crucifix dive
at Epiphany, when rain like a jeweler taps
gingerly into the crystal of a water crocus.

At five she was known as Mary Kalogeropoulos,
and if I could, I would tell her how my relatives
changed their amphibrachic name to Bass

gaining intelligibility despite melismatic loss,
the Slavic sonics of affricates and fricatives
(they pronounce it like the fish, not the tonal range, alas).

But her lossy name provides its own gloss.
Let mine underwrite hers like a bass line,
as though I had her otherworldly ear.

I attended to the Greek boys diving for their cross
as a girl released a white dove from the shrine
of her consecrated palms. We watched it disappear.

If Callas preferred to perform sans lenses,
leaving the concert hall a gold-vermilion blur,
was it to shield her conscience from the world,

so that she moved and sang in fictive stanzas?
Dives and songs that would disclose our nature
are from one held breath methodically unfurled.

Yes, here's a rump of Poseidon's kingdom.
In the gift shops, St. Michael spears the basilisk,
and Medusa rears her seething skull.

Some coral are classified as 'gorgonian'. Some
petrified bodies the treasure hunters frisk
might have been her victims, turned to marble.

The descendants of those divers will now dive
for the crucifix, in white tees, fresh from Mass,
processing barefoot down the main drag behind their priest.

A liturgical singer's baritone comes to us live
from the bayou's edge, where sacerdotal gulls amass,
and the modal melodies strike our ear as from the East.

They blessed the boats on Thursday at the docks.
By Friday, the wind was high, and late in the night
came torrents. To cancel a dive because of showers

creates an elemental paradox.
But here was the miracle: the rain took flight,
the clouds blew off at the behest of unseen powers.

Now the procession halted at the bayou,
and the priest took over from the singer – though
he wasn't singing exactly; but neither did he speak,

or rather, he spoke in circles, as rhymes do,
a sermon on water. That little of its flow
was in English, some diverted into Greek,

excited me like screams to the angelic orders.
For isn't a foreign language the beginning of terror?
May I ask the diva, if I briefly have her ear?

The boys leaped, and in the maelstrom, towards
the center, one surfaced. The crossbearer.
He was borne on shoulders back to the pier,

all handsome as cherubs halfway to turning seraphim.
The crowd erupted in applause. Meanwhile the terns,
facing the proceedings, crossed their wings

behind their backs. Their X'd tips had a darker trim,
as a soprano may have colors our ear discerns
when the language disappears in what she sings.

The Iliad in a Scottish Cemetery

The culinary garden on the burial grounds
raises a few eyebrows, but not the dead.
There's lovage, chamomile, pineapple sage.
The graven names are old Scottish names.
On my headphones, though, is *The Iliad*,
so my eyes take in Prestons, Grays and Grahams
as my ears do Agamemnon, Calchas, Diomedes.
On a plinth a bas-relief of storm-tossed seas
commemorates a mariner. The catalog of ships
survives in unfamilial polysyllables.
Names don't translate; a mouth of pebbles,
they slow the language roaring down the page.
I'm in two foreign countries at once, by turn
testing on my tongue the umami of these sounds,
iron-laced water like blood-anointed spear tips
and the tangy granite in the skirling burn.

The Mystery of Lovers Loan

'Look for the wyvern,' Chris told me. 'It's not on the maps.'
So I set off to find the secret footpath between high walls
snaking through the Grange. Isn't it bad enough these apps
leave me in dead ends, then drop their signals,
as when I was given a fenced-in graveyard as a shortcut?
The markers were taller than men, and everyone here knows
that stone is unpredictable. Rubble rebels, as in what
closed the Radical Road ('high risk of rockfall') and whose
'unconforming' nature changed the face of geology.
The avalanche sings austerely down the prominence
of the couchant volcano, a former flame. I came to see
this city reared itself out of sandstone – the wyvern's sibilance.

It's semiotically rich, a theorist would say: how the volcano
gives rise to the castle, a stronghold on the peak, while en face
across the Royal Mile sits the decorative pile where we know
soft power mounts a charm offensive – a woman's palace
with a physic garden. It was usurped from the monks
who made their peaceful anchorage in the lee of Arthur's Seat.
Bloodred rubies of Mary Stuart's rosary glitter as chunks
of history fall from the Abbey roof. Where the kings eat,
a holy stag set its flaming hoof. And where there's murder,
it's always in the chambers of the heart: the beds are soft.
Someone should have told Mary to be alerter
to the wyverns. Rocks can be scaled and fealty sloughed.

'Look for the wyvern.' So I go to the poison garden
where the belladonna is kept in cages, though the pollinator
roams freely in it. In fact, shadows, like a pardon,
widen their bee stripes on the path as the hour grows later
and hemlock vies with the castor bean's claim
to importance as assassin versus state executioner.
And now the owls and church bells utter the selfsame
chime, though not on purpose. Nor do the dead, I'm sure,
play chess except as two dates reach a stalemate.
The grammar of romance demands ellipses, perhaps . . .
as 'loan' for 'lane' gets at the glamour (same root,
in Scots) of a temporary state. It's not on the maps.

Foxglovewise

Whatever possessed me to climb the steep side
of Blackford Hill when such nice paths were laid
for us unathletic folk? Grabbing the gorse
with my bare hand, which had been electric gold
just two weeks ago; trampling on foxgloves
electric with bees – was this wise? Overlord
thistles, nodding to the vista, thistled steeples?
Signs warned against ticks bearing Lyme disease.
It wasn't reassuring that I still had it in me
to stray off the map – 'This is the hill she died on
. . . of a bee sting' – as it said on the ticket
in her raincoat pocket – 'off-peak single'.

Elegy and Bourbon

We live on a thin crust. I can hear
the Kentucky Derby on the wide-screen
     perched on its aerie
over the bar in terminal E. I can hear,
that is, the crowd-roar, the unseen
announcer's commentary,

but I can't hear the hooves. We live
on such a thin crust the horses
     could break through it.
I am three generations, give
or take, off the farm; history's forces
tear you by the root,

so no, I don't know a horse's gallop
from a canter. But that I can't hear
     their thunder makes me ponder
the thin crust we live on, a short drop
from the window, the runways that bear
aircraft touching down yonder,

the cracks spawned by their weight.
A whole city can grow in the fissures
     left by a volcano, the volcano
go dormant, a glacier scour its spate
of basalt, tectonic seizures
expose the devil's footprint: cloven.

Auden called it his 'Mutterland',
the limestone of the Pennine Chain.
    My limestone landscape has no
mountains, lies flat as a hand
on a Bible, pummeled by rain,
where plants that live on air can grow.

And then, over Jersey, the terrain
stretches outside my porthole
    all the way to the Delaware River –
this is where I've gone again and again
to bury my few people
in an Orthodox cemetery. Never

did inter my father's ashes, lost
when my brother had the house cleaned out.
    I cringe to think where
their resting place must be, tossed
in some landfill on his old commute.
And I didn't get my share

of their languages, either. This one
is all I have; its source has come
    to serve as my thin crust.
After I got the call, in London,
I stumbled up the back stairs of a museum
to see a mummy not yet gone to dust;

a whole roomful of dinner services
and tea sets. A higher order, for all intents
    and purposes dynastic.
The mint walls and the glass were cooling ices,
the ceramics like white-glazed patients
touched with tact in a hospital clinic.

Isn't porcelain made of the finest clay?
But piece by piece a family goes to pot.
    I pictured myself
a shard – earthenware to mislay,
liable to mislabeling in some entrepôt,
not on any museum shelf.

Such a thin shell we tread. Like an egg.
They pursue me to the gate, the silent hooves
    from a bar called 'The Explorer',
where I drink before my last leg.
I worry – so transient are my loves –
living on air, my words are poorer.

All Souls' Night

One sleepless night, something possessed me
to dig up the box I'd kept for thirty years
and lay out the wooden pieces, blond and ebony,
on the table, accounting for my chevaliers –

a real feat, after all the moves I'd made.
This was the set with which I learned to play,
the set that gave my dad and my mom's dad
a pastime during visits, on a holiday

when the TV von Trapp Family Singers
glossed the war that was their central fact.
These were the figures well worn by their fingers.
And for all my moves they're here, intact.

That night I also hunted down the Pushkin
my grandfather had, a haunted book
(it knows the ways I betray my origin)
preserving aspirational stanzas, whose look

on the page I liked too much to translate.
As with my family, what I couldn't understand
gained in fascination, verve, weight.
Cyrillic took on the features of its land,

but time is running out, the sun will flood
grace on a state I'll likely never see,
and the figures now revert to wood
at these words for the dead who raised me.

The Empire of Flora

A tossing garden in a rising wind,
an air of expectation. And Claire
tutoring me on the landscaping:
pagoda plants, crotons, a kind
of blue ginger; over there,
African lilies, bellwethers of spring.

When she points me to liriopes,
I expect the terrace to be inhabited
by a feminine miniature, nymph
or naiad out of ancient Greece
who makes a cushy, scented bed
for fauns, or Jupiter Himself.

I've forgotten that 'cerulean Liriope'
is the mother of Narcissus.
The Empire of Flora, Claire says,
is a disquieting kaleidoscope:
limbs, and hair, and faces
of those that love discountenances.

For – as if I needed reminding –
immoderate love comes to no good.
Claire is wearing a crisp white shirt.
To garden in? . . . Ah, she's rewinding
her lecture on Poussin, who could
take the measure of our hurt

and scale it to the interface between
roiling heavens and rock terrain.
Now instead of pointing out plants,
she's mapping the labyrinthine
myths of that famous picture plane:
Smilax sprawls on Crocus; Clytie pants

after Phoebus, but what she wants
to show me is the distancing
of Narcissus from close-seated Echo.
'Look at how desire taunts:
gazing is at right angles to listening:
that tells you all you need to know.'

The ear at right angles to the eye.
I never thought . . . and now the rain.
White-haired Claire in her shirt
(spotless, linen, practically a shroud) my
new garden cedes. Palmettos fan.
We put a frame around the dirt.

Art Tourism

Just as Jupiter spirited the girl to Crete,
this canvas was conveyed over the sea
and must surf its contradictions or drown.
(It looks as though Europa, her pose indiscreet,
should tumble onto us pretty heavily;
nothing ruffles the bull's flower crown.)

My memories of being young here
surface as a kind of automatism: lo,
my feet take over. Streets haven't moved,
buildings have stayed anchored. I hear,
as a couple kneels, pointing out a window
to their child: 'That's where we lived.'

Past the public garden (whose willows
are muscly!); past the 'Clock Repairs'
and 'Watch Hospital' – we're reminded
that turning back the hands throws
the interior mechanism into arrears
though not a minute is rescinded.

Past the public clock, then, and the chime
it wears in its funny hat. Once, the hours
had names and designated prayers;
now they're occasion for alarm, mere time
that at its leisure rubs out our powers
as we wear away the stone of subway stairs.

So: just as Jupiter spirited the girl to Crete,
this canvas was conveyed over the ocean
(and sails too were made of canvas).
We make pilgrimages, we pay tribute,
as its backward-glancing heroine
is a painter's tribute to a poet's stanzas.

We catch her at the end of her tour.
Her bodyguards are cherubs, armed
with arrows; even on our continent,
there's royalty. The princess of Tyre
has undergone restoration. Charmed,
vivid, and no less the frightened emigrant.

Supercell

East Texas

I'm waiting for this shrub to sew itself back in its soil.
Hearing its roots rip when I transplanted it made me quail
(though a cress or a lettuce remains my most favorite food).
A wind tore it up again, or it was undermined by flood.

Through the sorghum fields between Victoria and Lavaca,
a supercell, spurting electricity, smothered the ton of lava,
mounted in the sky, that characterizes sunset there.
But the tapestried sorghum fields created an atmosphere

that defied the monotony I associate with agriculture.
Planting, for me, means flowers – fitting embouchure
for birds; or aloes, answering to a sculptural imperative

to induce repose, and not just keep us, Lord, alive.
This hardy Duranta attracts hummingbirds *and* butterflies.
May it thrive, and sew itself in as the soil dries.

Between Victoria and Lavaca, in my mind's eye
I saw a thousand Comanche in cumulonimbi
racing thirty hundred stolen horses over the prairie
to the sea. When the sorghum field, that tapestry,

was little more than 'Chocolate Swale' (a sign stuck in the silt,
née swamp), official history passed the bolus of guilt
back and forth, from the Comanche, who kept back captives,
to the Texans, who (in what may have been an interpretive

blunder) slaughtered the chiefs, back to the Comanche,
who torched their captives in revenge and went on 'an orgy
of horse-thieving'. While at night Comanche jump

on Texas with a thump, the dream of one Buffalo Hump
results in enough calico and ribbon to get lost in
(as I sew myself into this clay) riding back to Austin.

Too late. Juliet Constance managed to get her hem wet
but they seized her and stripped her down to the whalebone
    corset
– flummoxed. While the townspeople watched from dinghies
    offshore,
on that hand-over-hand surf, helpless, they later swore

her whalebone wouldn't budge. They saw the town burning,
warehouses looted; and in the smoke's going and returning,
Comanche donning top hats and pigeon-tailed coats.
Adorned with all the brass buttons a merchant ship could
    float,

twirling their parasols and festooning each his horse
with ribbon, the Comanche departed. In the cumulonimbus
of their dust, they took our bibelot Juliet.

Buffalo Hump, meet Whalebone Corset!
For a gold watch her young husband perished. El Dorado:
where there's pyrite in the piranha, gilt in the sweet potato.

Gold in the sorghum tassels, gold in the sargassum weed
strewing the shore where they put Juliet on a stolen steed.
Gold when wet, that is; rust-brown when dry; furring the
    coast,
drying at different rates in the sun, so gold and rust co-roast.

It seemed a herd of buffalo was barbered by some god at first.
But in these alien bouquets tossed from the largest sea on earth,
and bounded by no lands, live animals find harbor.
Exquisite minnow worlds of crabs, shrimp – sheer automata –

crawfish cling to the tangle and grape ('sargasso').
I've seen the gulls in their tuxedo'd appetite clothed go
pecking there. Meanwhile, into an upended-frisbee'd

world my kids shake the bundles of sargassum seaweed,
collecting their own marine menagerie for observation.
The liverish waves play on, sunlight doled out in rations

from grape-stained clouds to whiten froth exploding
    in our ears.
A sulfurous wind blows in, then as suddenly disappears.
The deep blue, upended frisbee looks like nothing less
than a saucer of primal soup from Genesis,

the first meal of the first day. By the seventh all Creation
    and we
were invited to the feast of ourselves, into perpetuity.
She was saved a second time, that Juliet,
when a crop of arrows foundered on her whalebone corset.

Saved, then, with nothing more than a sunburn. And still
nothing more than a stone commemorating Linnville
between the new tract housing and the littoral.

Calico of wildflowers sewing themselves to the soil,
and a man licking his arrowhead, that his DNA be
shot through the heart as it pins her to the ponderosa tree.

A Midsummer Night's Work

Was it you, presenting in
the evening bougainvillea
as a hummingbird again,

voluptuary, dual
febrile wings ashine
as a seamstress's spool,

hovering over the bracts
with power tools to fix
a beam or caulk the cracks?

Was it you that soldered
one emerald frog
to its oleaginous polder

and a polyphemus moth
flattened like peanut-buttered
toast points on the footpath?

That espaliered to Orion
– bending backward –
one night heron?

Flamboyance

The lighthouse fruits like a bromeliad.
Its pineapple lens came from Paris.
It is named for an evangelist.

It stands like a majuscule, clad
above the glassy wilderness
in an ecstasy of coastal mist.

When you go there, don't expect
to see the flamingo right away.
Sky and bayou, calm as mirrors

hung too high to be checked
for your reflection, discourage display.
He wades at the center of rumor's

rippling circles, which he flicks,
standing on his honor, with one foot.
He has lost his flamboyance –

which is what we call flamingo flocks.
Knocked off his migration route
by that habitual annoyance,

a hurricane (or an archangel),
he's reconciled to doubt,
displaced by several lines of latitude.

He should be as easy to spot as a changeling
when the tide trickles out.
All the heartbreak you've withstood

has prepared you for this disappointment.
A prescribed burn smolders.
You can't tell if it's smoking or misting –

the visual field smeared as with ointment.
You'll reach for your binoculars
to catch fire and water coexisting.

Mermaids and Mangroves in Key West

You can pick up infections in such places,
which is why it's best to cuddle in a basket,
   like this one painted blue,
hung in marine-breeze green-gold spaces
where palm fronds are as private
   as peeking blinds, a loose-leaf view.

Yet when we step out (now it's your arm
I hang on), the air is thick
   and perfumed as an unguent.
It will not waft us to any harm.
A figurine Marlene Dietrich
   gave Hemingway as a present

leans on an Underwood – or is it
a Royal? – which polydactyl cats
   might take to tapping at night,
in the mansion they inherit
on behalf of conch aristocrats.
   What delicious novels they would write!

To be rich enough to own nothing, but bide-a-wee
in someone else's hideaway:
   that's their secret. They drink
treated water from goblets;
like hermit crabs we trade up sublets
   in the Sunbelt, in a lizard's blink.

After all, wasn't the 'last red cent'
spent on the pool set in cement
    to consummate the marital argument
just a pretty penny? The pool
in the banana grove's a jewel,
    but we're set already in a *mar azul*.

We drove the car over the Keys
as the Preludes and Fugues played.
    Music sluices through time;
nothing can hold the harmonies
just as the tide can't be stayed
    though it can turn on a dime.

A harpsichord string plucked
by a quill gives us goose bumps.
    Roosters comb through the gate
without permission. Usufruct
ensures that pleasure trumps
    property lines, deeds, probate . . .

(Street-level, the roosters make
a clatter of continual daybreak.)
    Up in the fronds, which crisscross
with every languid wind-toss,
one's own primate penchant
    swings to the tall and verdant;

butterflies in pairs contrive
magnetic pole dances, attracting/
    repelling on an invisible axis.
And almost as attractive:
a buzz without a sting,
    the slender-waisted Vespas!

Yet to discover, as we did,
a sailboat sunk in a mangrove
    named *Omega*, torpedoes
all illusions. I was reminded
of every beauty we disprove
    by drawing too close.

The green flag of 'Low Hazard'
was flying where we swam,
    but I felt the pull of the Gulf Stream,
warm, swift and not too, too far
from the horizon's flat-line cardiogram –
    there's hazard wherever there's a dream.

Each night the great refinery of sunset
leaves smoke and bilge in the sky,
    a cleanup job for seraphim,
and the bridges in silhouette
look like something left to fry
    on a power line. Slag of nimbus . . .

as smudgy cigars belie white yachts,
the flowers that look so smart on trees
    stub out, on the hood of my car
parked on the street, spots
of guano and sepal. Opera buffa, please –
    a light touch has taken us this far.

Think of the sphinx moth on the wing –
lured to the frangipani
    it pollinates politely. But it's not mutual.
The tree gets something for nothing,
the scent a 'false signal',
    no nectar but a perfume sample.

It will not waft us to any harm,
the breeze, and the clatter of keys
    might well be the fugues and preludes of these
polydactyl felines, with all the charm
of enclaves hugging their airstrips,
    wind socks buoying their spirits!

To My Hummingbird

paradoxical contrivances for intercrossing
— CHARLES DARWIN

ARCHILOCHUS COLUBRIS

From the red-light districts
of pomegranates
comes ruby-throated *Archilochus*

with his hocus-pocus metrics:
dithyrambs to Dionysus,
subsidiary of Zeus & Co.,

still fragrant from an imbroglio
involving Neobule.
Am I a sommelier

to provide miniscule
kraters for proboscises?
You whose juiciest papyrus

tells us you orgasm caress-
ing her hair – your iridescence,
erudite and crudité at once,

irreducible essence, registers
as with all megastars
as a contrivance: what orchids are

in the archipelagoes
where your fellow Apodiformes
evolved reciprocally.

Ergo when versifying sex
it is of coevolving one speaks:
the long metamorphoses.

Comes *Archilochus* again,
continually off-piste,
soldier, tough guy, making fun
of boys with hairdos
    all the while poking at the
C. *paniculatum*.

Why'd that Saxon taxidermist
give your name to something
    so dainty? –
your name must be thrilled.

Or maybe it was that
having ditched your shield
    to save your life

you must pay tribute
    to the smallest,
most defenseless of birds.

But you could only brag
about ditching your shield
because you could always
    afford a new one.

The only bird who can fly
forwards and backwards
wouldn't have a hard time
reading Greek papyri.
In these shady backyards
she could mend a rhyme

with Spanish moss and
spider silk, like the repairs
she makes to her own nest.
If she came on command
I wouldn't have to stare
so long with my nose pressed

to the window. But one day
she hovered there, in colors
jesters used to wear,
and teased me, as if to say
*Hey, princess, Archilochus
thinks you could use some fresh air.*

The Rain Trees

The rain trees are pink again.
They litter with a shrug,
unorthodox for October,

whose vintage is Keatsian,
clammy with muscat fug;
the rain tree's blush is sober.

In the north a torch is passed
from maple to oak to beech
as geese begin their processional;

the rain trees aren't classed
with myths we preach
of either the Idyll or the Fall.

A matte sound sounds like rain too –
rustling desiccants, seeds dehiscent
concuss on the gutters of the ear,

as Heaney with his rain stick knew.
Rain everywhere is heaven-sent
but rain trees portend dry months here,

flinging skirtfuls of potpourri –
soiled toe-shoe pink, muhly grass pink,
sow's ear pink, a silk purse made:

Can rain trees slake a parti pris
for elegy, for rain's right clink,
and claim spring's shade?

Madonna of the Oranges

In the backwoods and bayous
they grunt for worms in April:
it's a kind of chthonic festival.
The method that tortoises use

works for robins, and for folk:
thumping the ground, they claim,
fools the worms expecting rain.
(As if nothing else awoke:

after the bodies fall in Act V,
the actors stomp the boards,
resurrecting ladies and lords
before the worms arrive.)

Grotesque oranges fall since
huanglongbing went after citrus.
Madonna of Oranges, pray for us.
Psyllids bring the pestilence.

When orchards are obsolete forms,
will you sponsor an ubi sunt?
Will Floridian poets grunt
for elegies rather than worms?

Think of the scent gone forever.
Think of no orange blossom,
the loss to the sensorium,
the honey bee's chef d'oeuvre.

In greatcoat and red epaulet,
the blackbird croons a funeral.
Its breath creates a thermal curl.
As if to discharge the debt,

an orange thuds, summoning
breakfast for the early riser,
a worm, a phloem-colonizer,
an earworm, huanglongbing.

To My Guitarist

Did you ever think, when you cooed
over the delicate snails after rain,
or fed a lettuce leaf to your tortoise,
that your affinity for shelled creatures
revealed one of your own features,
a fear of being soft-bodied, porous,
lacking calcium carbonate or keratin
to house your defenseless solitude?

Those of us with hides like pachyderms
may find it harder to understand.
Remember how, at the turtle hospital,
you sobbed over old uses for tortoiseshell?
I feel it when I take your fretting hand:
the tenderness each callused tip affirms.

Chekhov in the Gulf of Mexico

The resort staff are turning off the light
at the poolside bar. The iron gate
around the pool clanks shut loud enough
to wake the kids whose sleep their mothers

toiled to obtain. This Saturday night
is uniquely musicless, the usual spate
of sounds drowned out – rough
and slick alike, proclivities and druthers.

Even the band abandoned their tunes
when the downpour came. Unwelcome guests,
clouds clash though you can't see the colors –

damson, plumbago, where the swimmer prunes
and lightning in a soft synaptic burst suggests
the heavens had a thought, which sank in the rollers.

In the morning another worker's come.
He brushes off the leavings of a palm tree
from the cushions with a pillow.
He cranks taut the skirts of the umbrellas,

so the colors resolve into a dome
of crisp stripes. He loops the ropes expertly
out of the reach of children, though
the overall look, from above, is of bull's-eyes.

Slashed fronds, slats, louvers, wickerwork –
when the breeze comes, everything's sieving.
Housekeeping the outdoors is an enterprise:

raking sand each morning like a Zen monk
so that the guests say, 'This is living.'
And the protected marsh is nodding, no surprise.

He puts the TV, she her face on.
A divorcée, with her teenage son
who mutters, almost immediately,
that the songs are all about pair-bonding.

Each song, she might reply, is a repetition
before it's a departure. But he's gone –
he notices the poolside palms surgically
relieved of their fruit. Tanning and blonding,

the guests make use of the green-banana light;
and maybe the umbrellas are really meant
to keep an epiphany from glancing off the skull.

When the sun climbs to a certain height,
a swish unwraps the cellophane from peppermint;
a green stripe in the surf burns auroral.

Tender the flesh under the shoulder strap,
and the bubble where the sandal thong chafes
threatens to burst. Sea grapes, saw palmettos.
A seraglio of interior paramours.

Little herds trot across the sand wrapped
in towels identical to the umbrellas. Waifs
wander in search of lizards. A man throws
out his arms: 'Venga, como una mariposa!'

and the little girl jumps. A boy, maybe four,
points out a baby iguana poking its snout
through the slats of a porch. The smallest

among us spot the minuscular. They adore
the giant chess set, knocking the queen out
with the flourish of a major plot twist.

Mother and son share a kayak. They bump
and bumble into the mangrove swamp
and barely keep up with the tour guide.
'Life starts here,' he's saying, 'the tide

brings animals and fish to incubate.'
Unsynchronously paddling the strait,
mother hissing, son throwing a backward glare,
they pantomime a mismatched pair.

Amid a cloud of kicked-up sand ('mermaid's milk'),
manatees, mouths full of seagrass, gleam in bulk.
The guide holds up a jellyfish; the boy puts out his hand.

A smile shows he's hooked. The sting he can stand:
it's impersonal. Now they sail through a cove
of hurricane wrecks and it looks like love.

Yes, the future has arrived to harass parents
while the scenery plays second fiddle
to the girls with cameras snapping – themselves.
The boy worships each one from afar.

The afternoon is turning a corner, hence
the heat, which makes the parking lot a griddle.
Better to languish on those balconies like shelves
than seek out the telescope which brings a star

too close. Besides, a starboard light will serve,
after too many rosé-colored glasses,
as the true purveyor of mysteries, because you know

there's a captain there, negotiating earth's curve.
Whatever the green light in the darkness promises,
what kissed you, you'll see in the morning, was a mosquito.

A steady stream of rhymes (lingo/gringo) purls
across the palms' scanty shade. Now country,
now reggae, now 'light contemporary'.
The balconies repeat dizzyingly, all rails

and wickerwork and cushions printed with zz's
receding like a single room between two mirrors.
A man, with his actress companion, appears.
The palms start up like a band in a sudden breeze:

rain, rain, rain, their only song. Crabs fallen
from the zodiac make like putts into their holes.
Rain, which drop by drop sounds a complaint

of zinc-tipped arrows against Eros, comes when
lightning collects its highway tolls.
Then we see what bull's-eye umbrellas meant.

The Mechanicals

'Couples can wed at the Miami Zoo . . .'
She is laughing to her confessor,
a tight-swathed, foiling hairdresser
(whose biceps playing peekaboo,

as he parts and lifts and snips,
suggest the weight of the flattening iron
or the tensility in the ringlets of that siren
chatting about her upcoming trips).

Zoe, meanwhile, creases my headdress,
also of foil, in which I look,
arrayed in silver, like a sci-fi Aztec
or Zoroastrian priestess.

Pop songs from the speakers gloss
the single, collapsible reason why
we cut, crimp, curl and dye:
lust, love, longing, and their loss.

'Do you know' – Zoe, suddenly begloved –
'that mad hatters were really a thing?
The poison they were absorbing
in their skin from doing what they loved

demented them.' She puts the timer on.
A second woman in black walks up,
and gives one of my hands a salt scrub.
It looks like she'll tell my fortune,

or no, like she's erasing the very lines
that map my destiny. 'All done . . .'
lifting her gaze; it's my complexion
she has read for unpropitious signs.

Dismantling the ziggurat, Zoe will remark,
'Airbags use a powder that leaves burns
when they're deployed. Funny what one learns,
sometimes, in this line of work.'

The Open C

You stare into it for days, all your life,
as if waiting for a curtain to rise. As if
a production of Ariel and Prospero
were pending in the ocean's void,
the amphitheater of the asteroid.
There's only shocked quartz below.
Where sky and sea are never parted –
there the mass extinction started.

Now resurface, to the serene
compact of our opening scene:
one blue mirror shows a poreless face,
dazzling evening's investigators.
The other, darker, on the case
reflects, close up, the craters.

The Missing Nymph at Dry Tortugas

A crown decayed or unfinished. Disarticulated bricks. An echo.

The cannons face the rolling breakers,
aimed at the line where sky and sea collude.
What do they defend? The wild enclosure,
which for two centuries has lived on rain.

Sixteen million bricks encircle sixteen acres.
There are no nymphs where there's no plenitude
of springs, although the sand's quite pure
that can't take the imprint of pain.

Here the sea disappears; through the premises
runs an inspissate whisper of tall grass
and low trees like kinked rope. What they meant

who can say, anchoring promises
of glory in the treasonous dunes? Alas,
the truth is there was never an engagement.

The truth is, there was never an engagement
that did not involve a ring like this brick ring
facing off against the sea. My favorite mystery,
as a child, was one where a missing fiancée,

heiress to a castle, had set her footprint in cement
near a fountain where Nancy Drew was trespassing.
Features of the imagination take on symmetry
from early exposure to gazebos, loggias – to ballet –

and the missing girl *was* a dancer. On the prowl,
Nancy Drew discovered the ruined gardens
behind the crumbling wall, so is it any wonder

I meander in a daze under keening seafowl,
and the ghost of a thousand rejected pardons,
to climb to the bastions just as I hear thunder?

Climbing to the bastions as it thundered,
I could take in the whole key. The terns cry,
circling their rookery. I stumble into the wind,
no guardrails. The sea opens a debris field

where the Spanish galleons foundered,
and the rumor of treasure comes to die.
Bejeweled reefs are the real find:
in a suspension of aquamarine, they yield

guardian angelfish around an ancient hull.
The Imperfect and the Historical Perfect, hence,
'serve to illustrate one another', I read in a lull.

The Ideal Conditional is the fanciful,
the Unreal Conditional the tragic tense:
'That which is Unfulfilled or Impossible.'

That which is unfulfilled or impossible
figures as this sea gale that batters the walls.
The tingle at the back of my knees tells me
to descend, back down the helical staircase,

which spirals to the ground like a shell,
and like a seashell or a mortar shell what appalls
is the idea of destruction embedded in beauty.
Yet the world is everything which is the case:

'Verbs of Reminding, Remembering, and Forgetting,
take the Genitive: *Ipse iubet mortis te meminisse deus*,
A god himself bids you remember death.'

The rain sails by and spares us; if I were betting
on the likelihood of rainbows, I would lose:
they're factored into sight by a hair's breadth.

Factored into sight by a hair's breadth,
or the turn of the tide, a shoulder breaking
the surface is just a shoal. No nymph. No
happy ending of disarticulated bricks.

The heiress fit her foot in the imprint beneath
the fountain, claiming the identity she'd forsaken.
(She'd broken her spine, gone incognito:
no more high-heeled spins and kicks.)

Iambs arose from marching feet, not dance
(says the grammar book). Here were convicts
and slaves. The fort is sinking peu à peu.

Bleak dry coral islet in the Gulf where by chance
I find a trailing vine of pink convolvulus
in whose trumpets lie, oh, tiny mutes of dew.

Th can on f ce t e roll ng br akers
                              . . . achers
wh ch for t o ce tur ies as l ved o rain
                              . . . reign
H re th se dis pp rs throu t e pr mi ses
                              . . . misses
w o c n sa anc ori g pr m ses
                    . . . says
fro earl e po ur to gaz b s, logg s – t ba let –
                              . . . lay
'Th   ich is Un ulfi led or Impo sible'
                              . . . sybil
whi h sp rals to the gr und like a she l
                              . . . hell*

---

* In a corner of the county library at Key West are stacks of deaccessioned
books for the taking. It's where I find *Latin Grammar* by Gildersleeve and
Lodge, published by Macmillan in 1895.

It is, no doubt, a Key to the West.

Aquamarine cloth cover, embossed letters – indigo, amethyst? – on the
spine. A binding sewn like canvas sails. A splodge of water discoloring the dye
had not progressed – errant student! – to blur the small print inside.

To arrive on this isle, it must have been shipwrecked. I wandered through
its pages like a treasure hunter: Interrogative Particles! The Accusative Supine!
Impersonal Verbs, where the agent is implied in the action: *It thunders. It
rains.*

I like verbs not only because they can be impersonal, but because like
weather they have moods. Something is *indicated*, *wished for* or *commanded*.

Prospero deploys the Imperative, telling Miranda – as we our works – 'Be collected'.

The Table of Temporal Relations promised Continuance, Completion and Attainment. 'Be Collected' dangles the promise of completion *and* attainment.

Causal sentences began: *Because – Now that – Since – it thunders*. Pure Final Sentences began: *So that – Thereby – it thunders*. Copulative and Adversarial sentences began: *But – it rains*. Copulation by Means of the Negative began: *And not because it thunders* . . .

Low-growing pines wrapped themselves, branches and roots, around unsupportive sand hills, as if in love (it will never last). The sand so pale was like kaolin, moon rock, bone dust. I heard a roar and I walked toward it. I went in flip-flops, in shambolic iambs over the dune (unlike 'ye that on the sands with *printless* foot do chase the ebbing Neptune . . .'). In the wind, the cautionary flags flew purple and red.

Adult Ballet

One returns, to forms of humility
that begin with relevé. And then
the teacher is younger than you.
The barre is anchored to mercury,
waists are ballasted by tutus. Resin,
darkening our soles with each tendu,

lends a hooflike realism to leaps.
Laddered tights climb like pretenders.
These slippers that seem so tiny
on the closet floor are shallops
('light sailboats used as tenders')
floating us to a strange neoteny.

Rosé, vin gris, gris de gris – a leotard
is the color of skin-contact wine.
The coolness is applied to parts in pain.
An earth sign, you believe in terroir:
vintages have horoscopes, or align
with transient bodies like comet champagne.

The need each of us has, to feel as though
we're the turning axis of a world,
rivets us to the mirror by our own gaze.
A severe expression replaces the glow
with which our faces were impearled
in what they call our 'salad days'.

One returns. Fantasies wear thin.
Late fall: evening and its leaf
and moss and mauve and bisque,
a mist as capacious as fiction
when suspension of disbelief
gives rise to a shaky arabesque.

Lowcountry

It's a working Christmas.
The container ships send me
a few lines from offshore.
Their string lights aren't arranged for
the purpose of festivity
but to mark the edge of the abyss.

Rain drills. In this monochrome
where an odd year prepares
to roll over to an even one,
something ominous or omicron
colludes in raising our fares
to send us definitively home.

It doesn't make sense to reach
for reading glasses when a tiny bird
swoops by, a blur so frantic
it seems that from across the Atlantic
comes, in pieces, a Greek word
assembling itself on a beach.

Hapag-Lloyd, Maersk, Hamburg Süd.
The rain drills. The crane swerves
over the scow, the clamshell dredge
plunges, and all the while the wedge
of the hull inwardly curves
for the maritime optics are odd.

Goods out of nothingness, fog,
or excelsior sail; a bridge sits
like the skeleton of a Sphinx
winking as the claw sinks.
Weighing mud and clay and bits,
progress keeps a faithful log,

for it's a working Christmas,
and the sea's gray eyeball
trembles like a dreaming sleeper;
it seems that, dredging deeper,
they might find a god, and haul
his swaddled marble to the surface.

Easter Mass Vaccination

In the event we forget the effect
of spiraling up the on-ramp
to expressways above the trees
where our eyes are wrecked
by sunlight bearing the stamp
of angelic principalities

and a hallelujah chorus
of so much chrome and mirror,
en route to the feculent parking lot
of a down-market, dubious
strip mall – where we'll bare
a shoulder (pick one) in a squat

Federal Emergency Management
Agency tent set up with tables,
folding chairs and electric fans,
whose roar is likewise giving vent
while we stick our printed labels
over our hearts. The barcode scans,

the flesh is swabbed and jabbed
by Navy personnel in camo,
surprise consideration in the gaze
above their masks. We're tabbed
and filed in seats row by row
for observation: Is what this says

that strangers are still good;
that when the stainless bandage falls
we are the beneficiaries, less of
new antibodies in the blood
than the ancient protocols
of principled and impersonal love?

Russian Fairy Tales

I felt a bit seasick with binoculars:
a device that captured my own trembling
as it enclosed a bird inside its egg.
Like dangling from cable cars.
Or glass-bottomed boats. Dissembling
abysses. Ibises that put out a leg
easily hatched from my field of vision.
Marjorie Rawlings and Hemingway
drank at the Moby Dick with a pioneer
of underwater film, Tolstoy's grandson.
That's what the little mullet had to say
when I leaned down and cocked an ear.

Voluptuous Provision

Ice storms shatter and varnish the South.
Up North, where my mother's housebound,
snow's furious refusal to fall wears out the wind
until it lies slack on swathes of earth.
South of the South – peninsula, on the map,
like a toe shoe pivoting on the Caribbean –
orchards shiver their aromatic snow, driven
by green rain and purple thunderclap
(and the subtle palpations of the bees)
until the ground approximates Paradise's
parody of winter. How good it smells, this
orange blossom. If anything could freeze
time into a crux of possibility and fruition
at once, it's this cluster of citrus
amid florets. I've been exiled *to* Paradise,
it seems: all seasons are now one.
Resurrection fern will grow in the groins,
lichen will pattern the trunk;
and where a harmless rat snake slunk,
silver moss will mint itself like coins
out of magical thin air. Production
is relentless, like the rain. Countrywide,
ice and snow cause pileups that slide
into the next life, but this goes on and on
like my mother's television, 24/7,
she dozing in its glare, the Jack Russell
curled on the daybed. Oh well,
when the pandemic is over, I imagine
nothing will have changed that much.
Her cake and cookie clippings will

all have remained aspirational,
gesturing at kitchen research.
And we will both have grown old.
How strange that the child who lay
in her young mother's arms can play
at their being contemporaries, as the cold
creeps south. Voluptuous provision,
keep me in your antic sight,
the ground of being underfoot,
fruit that mirrors back the sun.

Ringstrasse

I lost my grandmother's opera glasses . . .
an empire in thrall to innovations
offered electric shocks in the Prater
for a small charge. In wedding dresses,
fräuleins dove from moving trains. Scions,
following the Great Somnambulator,

walked out of windows (into Blush Noisette!)
or stepped off bridges in uniform.
Thunderclouds amassed
as if looking to discharge public debt
under the cover of a lightning storm.
It was on a day like any other that Albert Last

as played, perhaps, by a ringer for Strauss,
drowned. Baroness Vetsera (Louise Brooks)
descended from her carriage with a twirl
in front of the incandescent opera house.
No smelly tallow! She trained her binocs
on the Prince, a typical fangirl.

Yes, mine were the glasses that saw
coaches turn into pumpkins.
Fiacre – barouche – swagged and crowned.
Droshky – diligence – curricle – landau.
Phaetons, which for all their sins
never ran heaven into the ground.

Field Recordings in the 1930s

Here I am and where are you? – RED-EYED VIREO
Cover it up – BROWN THRASHER

We eavesdrop on the wheatear . . .
but when, in the buildup to war,
Ludwig Koch and his cohort stage
a mobile sound studio en plein air,
endeavoring to capture
not a nightingale, but its message,
is it a form of espionage?

And when we eavesdrop on the wheatear,
or, in the buildup to war, stage
a mobile sound studio en plein air,
endeavoring to capture
not a nightingale, but its message,
is it a form of espionage
because the nightingale ceases to sing
at the stylus furiously scratching?

As when we eavesdrop on the wheatear,
or, in the buildup to war, stage
a mobile sound studio en plein air,
endeavoring to capture
not a nightingale, but its message,
a form of espionage
when the nightingale ceases to sing
at the stylus furiously scratching
its wax cylinder, do we spook
at the thought that spies
are rife as the dragonflies
clipped to our neck of the woods?

As when we eavesdrop on the wheatear,
or, in the buildup to war, stage
a mobile sound studio en plein air,
endeavoring to capture
not a nightingale, but its message,
a form of espionage
because the nightingale ceases to sing
at the stylus furiously scratching
its wax cylinder, and we spook
at the thought that spies
are rife as the dragonflies
clipped to our neck of the woods,
does she betray herself to her enemies,
as when a team from Cornell, in 1932,
pitching a parabolic reflector in a meadow,
bounced a flycatcher's *qu'est-ce qu'il dit?*
toward shotgun mics
positioned at sonic foci?

So when we eavesdrop on the wheatear,
or, in the buildup to war, stage
a mobile sound studio en plein air,
endeavoring to capture
not the nightingale, but its message,
a form of espionage
because the nightingale ceases to sing
at the stylus furiously scratching
its wax cylinder,
betraying herself to her enemies,
spooking at the thought that spies
are rife as dragonflies
clipped to her neck of the woods,
like the team from Cornell who, in 1932,
pitched a parabolic reflector in a meadow,

does a flycatcher's *qu'est-ce qu'il dit?*
bouncing toward shotgun mics
positioned at sonic foci,
intercept the *whither-o-whither-I-flee?*
of the skylark?

Potatoes and Pomegranates

Winter had come to Nicosia,
and as the last daylight went,
braziers flared on the sidewalk.
In some language of Crimea
– or Medea – the men's heads bent
toward an ancient clock.

Was it a dream? I ate potatoes
'fluffy as a buttered cloud',
and sensed the red earth as 'read',
like Aphrodite's lips in the throes
of love: she mouthed aloud
the tale of grave Adonis's bed.

Earth apples, so-called, gather
the soil's nutriment into flesh
pale as moon rocks. They keep
in cellars, huddling together
in cool dampness to stay fresh.
Resistance in them runs deep.

(Just ask the knife that tries to
cleave them raw.) Age nine,
my orphaned grandmother was sent
to pick them in the fields and grew
into a figure unrelentingly benign
in a world that proved malevolent.

She was forgotten and trapped there
in the potato cellar for hours,
till someone discovered the error.
Entombed, then freed, she had a share
in rebirth, and now all bowers
had a whiff of pomme de *terror*.

Indeed, indeed, the seed I was
found itself inside her like a spud
the hour my mother's embryo
developed ova: by nature's laws,
dipped in the vitamins of blood
and coming to light like a memory.

Radishes

Smoke and ash of November.
A landscape of sediment and char,
lead and gold leaf, mutilated sod
racing on its planetary camber.
On a kitchen table's crude altar
a bowl of radishes is offered

with a dish of salt for dipping whole.
That's how my father would eat them.
My mother sliced them thin.
Theirs was no house in a fairy tale.
Yet the knife that trimmed the stem
and scraped the blemished skin

would halt at her intrepid thumb.
Radishes of rosy cheeks, of snow,
peppery radishes of yesteryear,
which made my tongue go numb,
why are you so much milder now?
You don't set the mouth on fire.

Did something in your cultivation change,
or does sensation wane with age?
In a French film, I saw two friends
spread butter on radish halves; strange,
I thought, but now it's all the rage
to sauté them. Their trailing ends

clog my drain stopper. Best is raw:
it's 'war' backward, like a spell
grown in the cold ground, color
of rose and snow – good to gnaw
a vegetable so filial and feral
late in the year, when the knife is duller.

The Stars over Red Rocks

Now you see, Urania, where the amphitheater was.
They built it, like the ancient Greeks, all open plan.
Provisioned with natural acoustics, the space between
the two largest outcrops accommodates a crowd

and brackets the constellations; Cancer's claws
grasp heaven as the wind from Saskatchewan
pours unstoppably through this pass, a scene
straight out of the fragment of that poem plowed

from the ruins of the library, fragment fifty-three:
'The Big Dipper reached down to scoop the music
but only sieved it.' It also has that image
of all the women's hair lifted streaming in the wind . . .

These boulders are untouched, virtually,
in the thousand years since she dropped the mic.
Two pianos faced each other on the stage:
the tilt of the lid propped open on the baby grand

echoed that outcrop there.
                              Professore   did
they bury the instruments with their divas   I'm thinking
of the lyre found in the grave of Queen Puabi at Ur

Or the horse buried with his warrior!
That's the truth those Bösendorfers hid:
that they were Trojan horses, keys plinking
amiably until a chord change – ruse de guerre –

and then they were attacking, an archetypal force.
Hardly entertainment. Why do you think that lyre
was decorated with a lion-headed eagle,
a man with a bull's head and horns? Leopards

and gazelles? Lapis lazuli and gold they'd source
from mines and rivers were thought to inspire
divine song; instruments had to be regal
like the painted cabinetry of some clavichords

depicting mythological contests between gods
and hapless satyrs. These people weren't known
to embellish their instruments the way they tattooed
themselves, but little was handcrafted in those days . . .

Each act, each performer sought – what are the odds –
the fulcrum to move these rocks, said to groan
and thrash and sob, such was the magnitude
of Orpheus's gift for lamentation and praise.

See the angle of that jib, that cross-sectioned cone
of turbiditic sediment crushed by its own pressure
then subducted so it stands almost vertical?
And then the oblate boulders like dinosaur eggs?

The earth blushed here. *Well   it is an orogenesis zone*
Touché, Urania. Can Muses be funny? *Sure*
but while you were thinking me your pupil
trying to teach me Time   I was thinking miles and legs

fathoms and versts and parasangs   I'm farsighted
as a seasoned mom   but Time   Professore   forget it.
I see in long frozen exposures   like an early camera
your eras are mirages   acts mirages of an era

Orangerie

Sometimes I think I must have ground to a halt
on this lot for the sake of the orange tree alone.
I might have preferred the olive – rolled
on a bias – but it requires labor, refinement, salt.
Oranges are easy: sweetness sewn
   inside a roughly perfect handhold.

Fruit in different stages of production muscles
the bough into a bow, the bow into a lyre,
plucked string lengths sounding a golden mean.
They long to dispense their light in bushels,
these overburdened arms; as they grow higher,
   they find my roof, on which they lean,

and then the spheres go reeling like billiards
down gutters angled like a kinetic sculpture–
cum–candy dispenser. Think how pretty!
Think if you were a house, contemplating yards,
wouldn't you choose one with a culture
   of citrus, the least complicated beauty,

to run aground on? That is, if houses,
like arks, sailed from firmament to foundation.
This tree is a juggler drawing out his long game.
Inspired, I swap my bow for sternness.
It is serious, this groundless elation.
   C'est mon bijou, mon or, mon âme, my name.

The Cemetery of Pseudonyms

Where do stargazers go in a city of light?
  Here, where shadows draw back
    lids on the abyss. Where trees raise a toast,
blossoms brimming, to the height
  at which a note will crack.
    Where it's your word against – your dust.

The area initially seems too small
  to accommodate so many pharaohs
    and consorts. Reduced as an amphora
to its handle, the person after all
  may be shelved neatly in rows
    and archived in the font of her era.

Up, down and across: the crypts
  feature midcentury names
    which used properly to be faces –
and typed, at that. The scripts
  graven into plates have the same
    effect as an iconostasis.

As though this were a tumulus
   accidentally excavated
      where parking was planned,
the empty flower sconces
   look like libation flutes that sated
      the gods with a tip of the hand.

Note the burial of the burial ground
   inside a city block, incognito;
      din of traffic, sunlight
enough for a star to hide in. Are we bound
   to the soil we're *born* or *consigned* to?
      Or do we root in the air like an epiphyte?

Those unplanted plants – they would be
   like words whose roots trail into myth,
      a mixed medium, no monolith.
Likewise our souls are in our names, which flee
   the gravestone, and like the moth
      invent themselves out of whole cloth.

It is none other than Apollo driving a yellow
   SLK 320 on the 405; when
      I see him again, at the Getty
('Our Acropolis,' you said) I am slow
   to absorb the lesson I am given:
      'A god's name has no etymology.'

Acknowledgments

Grateful acknowledgment is due to the editors of the journals and websites in which these poems first appeared: *The American Scholar*, *Bad Lilies*, *Liberties*, *The London Review of Books*, *The New Republic*, *The New York Review of Books*, *The New Yorker*, *The Paris Review*, *Revel*, *The Southern Review*, *Tourniquet Review*.

'The Open C' was selected for inclusion in *The Best American Poetry 2024*. Many thanks to editors Mary Jo Salter, David Lehman and Mark Bibbins.

Dedications: 'Art Tourism' is for David Mikics. 'To My Guitarist' is for my son, Gray McNamara. 'Russian Fairy Tales' is for Boris Dralyuk. 'The Cemetery of Pseudonyms' is for Stephen Yenser, with thanks for guiding me to the Pierce Brothers Westwood Village Memorial Park and Mortuary, a.k.a. Sunset Cemetery.

'. . . like screams to the angelic orders. / For isn't a foreign language the beginning of terror?' adapts the opening of the first of Rilke's *Duino Elegies*.

'Supercell' derives in part from an anecdote in *Empire of the Summer Moon* by S. C. Gwynne.

'*C'est mon bijou, mon or, mon âme*, my name' adapts a line from Wallace Stevens's 'Sea Surface Full of Clouds'.

Warm thanks to Jonathan Galassi, Katie Liptak and Oona Holahan at Farrar, Straus and Giroux, to Lavinia Greenlaw, Lavinia Singer and Hazel Thompson at Faber & Faber, and to Sarah Chalfant, Luke Ingram and Jacqueline Ko at the Wylie Agency.